# Unleashing
## *the*Mother
## *in* You.

## S. Musa Korfeh, Sr.

ELEVIV PUBLISHING GROUP
Houston, Texas 77082

Published By Eleviv Publishing Group, Houston, Texas
www.elevivpublishinggroup.com
1-713-548-3184

Book Layout & Art Direction: Nestto Graphics
Cover Design: Nestto Graphics

Photographer:

Printed in the United States of America

# DEDICATION

To my beloved mother, Mary Kaiuway Cooper, and my wife Farmah, you are highly favored amongst women.

To the women of Bethel Houston.

To all the women who have never had children, but have mothered and are mothering the children of other women by caring, supporting, feeding, guiding, educating, and adopting them.

# ACKNOWLEDGEMENT

There are many people I would love to extend my gratitude to for all their support in making this book a reality. First, to God almighty, without whom I am nothing.

To my darling wife and the mother of my children, Mrs. Farmah Jereldine Korfeh, I love you. Thank you for teaching me about love, life, possibilities, and what God's heart towards me feels like. Thanks for your ideas when writing this book.

To my mother in law, Mrs. Pearl Sackie, the woman who taught me about the beauty of motherhood, thanks for being a wonderful grandmother to my children. I love you always.

To all the women in Bethel Houston, as I lead you, I learn more about myself and what God has called me to do. You have taught me the true meaning of service.

To Bishop Darlingston G. Johnson, you have been a

beacon of light, and as I follow Christ, I look at you. Thank you for your prayers.

To my children may you grow up to be everything your mom and I envision for you to be. I love you.

To Dr. Lychene Saah, thank you for your support and prayers.

To Mrs. Phanta Martta and Sister Hervee Kpi, thank you, and may God continue to bless you.

To Tina Amadi, you have been a great support before, during, and after the publishing of this book. I know this is just the beginning (You have a story to tell the world).

To my publisher, Vivian Elebiyo-Okojie, thank you for your help and encouragement in making this project successful.

# COMMENTARY

Unleashing the Mother in You, is an enlightening and insightful book by Rev. S. Musa Korfeh, founder of Power Ministries International. Through the pages of his debut book Korfeh walks us through the life of Moses and shows us how God equipped each woman to play a unique role of a mother in his life. He challenges every woman to recognize that she is similarly gifted and to embrace that challenge as God presents the opportunity. This book is a model that will help women broaden their understanding of motherhood as more than a biological assignment but a God-ordained gifting and calling to be embraced for God's purposes.

**Diane Tezeno**

Pastor S. Musa Korfeh, a man full of God's divine wisdom has skillfully produced a rich and enthralling masterpiece. His wealth of knowledge and experience have been masterfully intertwined throughout the pages of this book buttressed by compelling testimonies and illumination by the Word of God.

Thematically arranged, "Unleashing the Mother in You" urges and challenges all females to serve as a "motherly figure" to our younger generation. Thus, we can all plant seeds of love, devotion, generosity, prayers, forgiveness, and encouragement in the lives of others. This revolutionary book is a must read for all!!

**Lychene N. Wolo Saah, Ph. D.**

*(Mother, Scholar, Mentor, Counselor)*

# TABLE OF CONTENTS

DEDICATION     III

ACKNOWLEDGEMENT     IV

COMMENTARY     VI

FOREWORD     XI

INTRODUCTION     13

CHAPTER 1:
THE WOMAN ON A MISSION     17

CHAPTER 2:
THE MOTHERS IN MOSES' LIFE     27

CHAPTER 3:
MOTHERS IMPACT DESTINIES     65

CHAPTER 4:
THE CALL TO MOTHERHOOD     75

ABOUT THE AUTHOR     87

# FOREWORD

Without doubt, the most important job on earth is the job of a mother. Nothing else can compete. It begins nine months before a child is born and continues in one way or the other as long as both mother and child are alive. And it's a job only a woman is equipped to handle! Unfortunately, today the importance of motherhood is being diminished. Stay-home Moms are viewed by many as inferior to their counterparts who prioritize professional careers. Women are made to feel that they are not successful unless they can compete in the marketplace and do, as well as, or better than men. The unfortunate result of buying into this false notion of success is that less and less time is being given to the most important assignment on earth--mothering!

Mothering is far more than giving birth. It is much more about nurture. It is the ability and the art of caring for, protecting and encouraging the development and growth of people. It transcends biological boundaries.

In his book, Unleashing the Mother in You, Rev. S. Musa Korfeh recognizes the unique gift of motherhood bestowed upon all women. He challenges women to acknowledge this gift, cultivate it, and employ it effectively. He knows that the future of the Church and of the world depends heavily on how well women execute their responsibilities to mother the next generation.

Using several examples of godly mothers in Scripture, Rev. Korfeh was able to illustrate biblically what can happen when women decide to release the mother in them. The women he highlights are not limited to biological mothers only. His argument is that every woman has the potential to mother others, and that all women should embrace this role enthusiastically.

My prayer is that women everywhere will hear and receive the message of this book. And that they will arise like never before to fulfill their unique role. May they see how their gift of motherhood holds the key that can release dormant potential locked up in the hearts and minds, not only of the children they give birth to, but of God's children everywhere.

**Bishop Darlingston G. Johnson, M. Div., D. Min, D.D.**
*Presiding Prelate, Bethel World Outreach Ministries International*

# INTRODUCTION

Mother's Day 2011, is a Sunday we will never forget. In our 25 years of ministry, we had always scheduled a guest preacher to deliver the message, but on this particular Mother's Day we had not done so. As we sought the Lord for a Word the night before, we sensed the Lord stirring our hearts to study and meditate on the birth of Moses. During our study, we received by revelation that the women God placed in Moses' life were divinely called to serve as mothers in order to preserve his life for the greater purpose of God. As we read and studied the first and second chapters of the book of Exodus, it became clear that Moses' biological mother could not have delivered him safely without the divine role, obedience, and ministry of the Egyptian midwives.

Secondly, we understood, by the Spirit of God that Miriam and Pharaoh's daughter also were positioned by God and their actions were ordered by God to preserve Moses and prepare him for his destiny. As a result of this revelation, we titled the message, "The Mothers in Moses' Life." We did not fully appreciate the impact the

Word had on the church until Monday morning, the day after, when one of the mothers who received the Word, Deaconess Phanta, and my wife, Pastor Farmah, asked me to consider writing a book on the message. After about six months, we began the project. We hope this book will bless all the women who read it.

In our message, we stressed over and over that every woman has a mother in her and is created and gifted by God to mother a child, biological or adopted. We asserted that a woman is not a mother simply because she has given birth to a child. As we delivered the Mother's Day message, the emphasis was placed on this truth. Many children grow up in homes without a biological mother, only step mothers. One young man shared his experience with me. "My father was a polygamist. He married several women and divorced them as they became incompatible. It is difficult to forget the loving and caring mothers and not cherish every moment of the love I received from them. Here is the truth based on our experiences, "Every woman carries a mother in her that is capable of loving and caring for a child, biological or adopted."

As a woman, believe that there is a mother in you. You need to release that mother in you. This book is an encouragement to every woman to release the mother in her by caring for an orphan, your stepchild or the child in your neighborhood that needs a mother's love and care.

There are young men and women who grew up with loving step mothers who cared for, nurtured, and raised them as though they were the biological mothers. They are thankful to these women who mothered them as they journey towards fulfilling the plans and purposes of God for their lives. There are many women who had the opportunity to love, care for and support the children that God placed in their care, but they did not, simply because they were not their biological children. Some ill-treated their step children and gave little or no love and care when they could have done more. Sad to say, they only love and care for their own children and the husband.

As you read this book, the story of Moses' birth, his difficult beginning, and the possible death sentence he faced as an innocent baby, please note that the Egyptian midwives, his sister Miriam and the daughter of Pharaoh were called and positioned by God as mothers alongside his biological mother, to mother him at different point of his life to fulfill God's purpose for Moses' life. Stop and look around you for the opportunities you currently have to mother a child.

**Be blessed and empowered as you read;** *Unleashing the Mother in You.*

# CHAPTER 1

# THE WOMAN ON A MISSION

Women are God's most wonderful creatures. They are the tenderness of God's heart, the reflection of His beauty. I believe God created women to show us His role as a parent. The Bible is laced with several stories of women who beat the odds, worked for God, and gave birth to amazing children. A mother is the Bible's most honored woman, and the Bible talks a great deal about her influence. Like Mary, the mother of the Lord Jesus Christ, who is the world's most revered mother, and her cousin Elisabeth, who gave birth to John the Baptist. Salome was another great woman and mother in the Bible. She was the mother of the disciples, James and John. She and her sons were very close to Jesus. She was very ambitious and was determined for her sons to enjoy extra prestige during Jesus' ministry.

Matthew 20:21 says, **"Grant that these my two sons may sit, the one on thy right hand and the other on the left, in thy kingdom."**

Jesus rebuked her gently in verse 23 as follows: **"To sit on my right hand, and on my left, is not mine to give, but it shall be given to them for whom it is prepared of my Father."**

Salome evidently handed down a rich spiritual legacy to her sons. It was to her son John that Jesus entrusted His own mother at the end. And it is commonly agreed that James was the first apostle to be martyred. Apostle Paul loved Timothy as if he were his own son. He writes to him in II Timothy 1:5, saying, **"I call to remembrance the unfeigned faith that is in thee, which dwelt first in thy grandmother Lois, and thy mother Eunice; and I am persuaded that in thee also."**

Eunice and Lois seem to step right from the pages of the Bible to tell us that nothing is more important in a mother's life than the early training of her children. We can be sure Timothy was vast in the knowledge of the Old Testament, the book of Judges and the wisdom in Psalms and Proverbs. Timothy was only about fifteen when he left them to go with Paul and Silas to preach the Gospel. Hannah of the Old Testament when she left her young Samuel in the House of the Lord at Shiloh, said, **"I have lent him to the Lord; as long as he liveth he shall be lent to the Lord."** (I Samuel 1:28)

Hannah had named her son Samuel, meaning, "asked of the Lord." She had prayed for his birth and made a promise that if she was rewarded with a son, she would consecrate her child to God. Then when he was about three years old, she took him to Eli the priest for training.

Rachel, mother of Joseph and Benjamin, was the first woman on record to lose her life in childbirth. Rachel died when Benjamin was born. Benjamin must have heard a great deal about his mother because Jacob loved her dearly. The second on record to lose her life in childbirth is an un-named mother, mentioned briefly in I Samuel 4:19-22. She symbolizes the woman who gives birth to a child after she has received word of her husband's death in battle. She also symbolizes the mother who succumbs to dark, despairing hopelessness. She named her child, Ichabod, saying, **"The glory has departed from Israel."**

Another woman was David's favorite wife, Bathsheba, who was a remarkably powerful woman. After falling into the sin of adultery and subsequently losing her son, I am sure she sought God with a contrite heart and went from despair and a life of sin, to become the mother of Solomon, the wisest man and king who ever lived. She intervened to have Solomon succeed his father as king.

Rebekah's life ended with her becoming a frustrated heartbroken mother. She brought about hostility between her twin sons, Jacob and Esau. She was on a mission as well to see one son succeed the other. Although her motives were all wrong, she exemplified the extent a mother would go for the betterment of her child. The first mother, Eve, experienced all the anxieties, heartaches and torments suffered by other mothers of wicked sons down through the centuries of time. Her first and most beloved son, Cain, killed his brother, Abel. Much later, a son was born named, Seth, as well as probably other sons and daughters whose names are not listed. She lived on in Seth, the strongest of her children.

The ancestry of Jesus Christ was traced back to the line of Seth. Abraham's beloved wife Sarah was a Mother of Nations. She suffered the pain that a woman feels from barrenness and for years she wept because she wanted to give her husband a son in fulfillment of God's promise. Her son, Isaac, was born in her old age, the Bible's first story of a miracle conception. Sarah emerged as a woman of power, one who was a dutiful and beloved wife and who finally became a favored and venerated mother. There are several women in the Bible, like Deborah, Sapphire, Jezebel, the woman at the well, Martha, Mary, Potiphar's wife, the widow, and so on. Some names stand out as women who did exploit for God and others for their wickedness. There are 188 named women in the Bible. The word 'mother' appears in the Bible almost 300 times. The phrase "And his mother was..." appears 20 times in II Kings and II Chronicles. The phrase underlines the importance attached to the mothers of kings.

For the purpose of this book, we will be focusing on the women who played a role in the life of Moses. Women, like Miriam, his sister, Pharaoh's daughter, his adopted mother, Shiphrah and Puah, the midwives who helped save his life, and finally, Jochebed, his birth mother who had the wisdom to protect him from Pharaoh's soldiers.

Jochebed was the mother of Aaron, Moses, and Miriam. Her name lives on, not by how many big things she accomplished, but by how wisely and well she served as a mother. For the first three months of his life, she kept Moses hidden. I can't even imagine how difficult it was for her to keep a noisy and squirmy baby hidden for that long. Then she wove an ark of bulrushes and put Moses in it, and placed him in the right current of the river so that someone else could get him. When Pharaoh's daughter sought a nurse for the child, it was Jochebed who was given the task of caring for him until he was seven. Perhaps we can trace in the peculiarly gentle character of Moses the influence of this devout mother.

A mother's influence is also stressed in Ezekiel 16:44 where we read the phrase, "As is the mother, so is her daughter." The love of children was deep in the hearts of the Hebrew women, and the mother was regarded with the deepest reverence. A quote by Abraham Lincoln, says "All I am and hope to be, I owe to my mother." The seriousness of a woman, when committed to something, is unexplainable. She is highly passionate and highly committed. When a woman is committed to a task, regardless of the challenges, she puts her all into it. In the case of the women who influenced Moses' life, they were committed to the cause. They were ready to die for that commitment. From my experience as a pastor, when a woman is given a responsibility she's up for the task, but men when given the same tasks lag behind. That is why I believe God entrusted women to the tasks of being mothers, carrying a child for 10 months in the womb, the pain of labor, and the eventual care of that child.

Women in general take their mission seriously, even in the secular world; women are committed to their homes, children, and husbands. They take their assignments seriously; they perform their assignments with all seriousness and commitment. No wonder there are more women than men in churches all over the world. They are committed. It is my opinion that because women take their mission seriously, God calls them and entrusts them with extraordinary responsibilities. God also knows the seriousness a woman attaches to her call in life; not only to deliver a son like Moses, but children in general, and to keep their commitment and fulfill their calling.

The women in this book took their mission seriously; they were committed as entrusted by God. A woman is a mother, a help meet, a teacher, and a provider. A woman will wake up to take care of a crying newborn, while her husband snores through the night. "We are just not built for that." But I believe more and more men should help out with the care of their children.

Perhaps the most important aspect of this book is the amount of faith and courage all of the women possessed. The intuition and perfect timing of Pharaoh's daughter, the persistence of Miriam, his sister, Jochebed's courage and faith in becoming pregnant after the decree was made about children. Shiphrah and Puah feared God; they obeyed God instead of the king's command in saving the lives of the children they delivered. I believe a woman must utilize every opportunity to impact a child's life, whether or not she's the mother of that child. Timing is very important, and every one of these women made sure their timing was impeccable.

Intuition is also important; women have an innate ability to sense things. Let God guide your steps in your everyday journey. Pharaoh's daughter had the intuition to go bathe in the river, where she saw baby Moses. Jochebed followed her intuition as she hid baby Moses for three months. She was resourceful and calculative. The midwives fulfilled their mission. God placed them strategically and Pharaoh could not change their minds, even in the face of death.

When we do what God asks of us, in the face of calamity,

He blesses us in return. A woman must be able to stand up for what is right, a mother must be able to sacrifice, even her own life, for the truth.

Women in general are endowed with the grace of God that equips them to not only conceive and give birth to children, but also to have the ability to care for, protect, and nurture children. Whether or not a child is a woman's biological child, I believe a woman is apt with the ability to mother that child.

My word of encouragement to you as a woman who has not given birth to your own child, regardless of that fact, the truth is that you are a woman gifted by God with the ability to mother a child, biological or not. Yes, you are a mother. Every woman has a mother in her. That woman in you is gifted to protect, provide for, nurture, encourage, empower, deliver from danger, educate, supervise, and care for a child.

Look inside and beyond you, then you will see the caring and loving mother you were made to be. Look for the opportunity to mother a child who needs a mom. When you begin to play the role of a mother in that child's life, I believe God will give you the peace and joy of a mother you have never experienced before.

While I was in Bible College, a good friend of ours got married. The woman was beautiful inside and outside; she was a very strong woman, she was also loving, and caring.

As her friend, we knew that she would make a wonderful wife and mother for the brother and his children. She was a very good cook and was very hospitable. Recently when we travelled for our ministry's General and International Conference, we spent time with them; and we saw how much they loved children and cared for others. We knew that they wanted to have and raise their own children. They were very active in our local church. They are active members, faithful tithers, and givers to the work of God. They began to pray and believe God for children. For many years, they believed and waited on God for children. Then the couple decided to adopt a child. He was a beautiful baby boy, fair in complexion, just like both of them.

If you saw him with them, you would have thought he was their biological child. One, because of the way she mothered, cared for, dressed, protected, and nurtured him. Secondly, he looked just like them in complexion. Several years passed, and the parents of the child decided they wanted their son back. They were heartbroken, especially the wife. They did not fight back, because it was a relative, they decided to give back the boy to his biological parents.

After ten years of waiting, God blessed them with three beautiful children. God answered their prayers and the prayers of friends, and family members. Today they have three beautiful and wonderful children, two boys and one girl.

It is my firm belief and conviction that God turned her shame and disgrace around when she allowed and released the mother in her, in caring, nurturing, protecting, etc. in practical ways as an adopted mother to the boy. As a faithful woman of God, she accepted the mission to mother someone else's son, and by doing so, the mother in her surfaced and manifested. We and many others saw the fruit. She took care of him as her own child. You would have never known that he was adopted unless she or someone told you. The three bonded so well that in my estimation, they became a perfect family.

As a well-mannered, disciplined, and dedicated woman of God and wife, her motherhood was one of discipline and dedication to her son. He was well taken care of and nurtured spiritually as well as physically. In the scriptures, we are told to do all things as unto the Lord, which always brings glory to God. She, becoming a mother of three, is a living testimony to the power of the living God and His ability and power in making the impossible, possible. Because she allowed the mother in her to emerge, God allowed her the joy of motherhood by giving her biological children.

# CHAPTER 2
# THE MOTHERS IN MOSES LIFE

As mentioned earlier there were so many women in the Bible who affected the lives of their children in one way or another. For the purpose of this book, I will focus mostly on Moses. He was influenced by so many women, and as we all know his life was significant and still is.

## JOCHEBED: THE MOTHER OF MOSES

Moses' biological mother, Jochebed, models for women an example of a woman of God and a woman of faith. She was a woman of faith because in the face of possible death, she did what was unthinkable and senseless given the circumstances and Pharaoh's decree. A woman of God because she did not fear man, the King of Egypt, and pursued wisdom as she protected her son from the slaying of that time. She sacrificed her very freedom to preserve the life of her son, Moses.

The scripture does not say much about Jochebed, however; what we read about her is enough to convey her character and tenacity. We will look at the passages that directly and indirectly mentioned her with the hope of exploring and gleaning from her godly life. We can learn so much about Jochebed's faith and be inspired by her strength and courage; a revelation that will challenge every Christian woman to trust God, as she discover and fulfill her God-given purpose in life, which is to become a mother. We want to look at Jochebed's life, mission, and the reward of her faith in Christ.

## JOCHEBED'S LIFE

In Exodus, chapters 2:1-10, 6:18-20, 15:20-21 and Numbers 26:29, we read about her life, and her faith.

1. Now [Amram] a man of the house of Levi [the priestly tribe] went and took as his wife [Jochebed] a daughter of Levi.

2. And the woman became pregnant and bore a son; and when she saw that he was [exceedingly] beautiful, she hid him three months.

3. And when she could no longer hide him, she took for him an ark or basket made of bulrushes or papyrus [making it watertight by] daubing it with bitumen and pitch. Then she put the child in it and laid it among the rushes by the brink of the river [Nile].

4. And his sister [Miriam] stood some distance away to [b] learn what would be done to him.

5. Now the daughter of Pharaoh came down to bathe at the river and her maidens walked along the bank; she saw the ark among the rushes and sent her maid to fetch it.

6. When she opened it, she saw the child; and behold, the baby cried. And she took pity on him and said, this is one of the Hebrews' children!

7. Then his sister said to Pharaoh's daughter, Shall I go and call a nurse of the Hebrew women to nurse the child for you?

8. Pharaoh's daughter said to her, Go. And the girl went and called the child's mother.

9. Then Pharaoh's daughter said to her, Take this child away and nurse it for me, and I will give you your wages. So the woman took the child and nursed it.

10. And the child grew, and she brought him to Pharaoh's daughter and he became her son. And she called him Moses, for she said, because I drew him out of the water.

The above text does not mention Moses' mother and father's name. It simply says: "And there went a man of the house of Levi, and took to wife a daughter of

Levi." However, it is obvious that reference is to Moses' biological mother and father. Other passages that we have considered in our discussion mentioned her name. In Exodus 6:18-20, his name is mentioned as Amram. The text revealed that he is a son of Kohath and a Levi. Exodus 6:20 says this:

> "AMRAM TOOK JOCHEBED HIS FATHER'S SISTER AS WIFE, AND SHE BORE HIM AARON AND MOSES; AND LIVED 137 YEARS."

And in Numbers 26:59, we read the following:

> "AMRAM'S WIFE WAS JOCHEBED DAUGHTER OF LEVI, WHO WAS BORN TO LEVI IN EGYPT; AND SHE BORE TO AMRAM, AARON, MOSES, AND MIRIAM."

All of the above scriptures paint a picture of the life of a woman of God, the mother of Moses, Jochebed. She is said to be the daughter of Levi, taken as wife by Amram, a Levi himself. She was born to Levi, raised in Egypt, and educated in Egyptian culture and customs; however, she was raised in the fear and knowledge of God because she is of the priestly tribe, Levi.

In today's language, we would say she was born and raised in the Pastor's house or in a Christian home. Some would even call her a Pastor's kid (PK). If this is true, then we can deduce that she was taught the law (scriptures) and faith in God and His Word. From all indications, and considering the plan of God for Israel in Egypt, she must have been a decent and beautiful young lady. Is it any wonder that she was taken by Amram? Exodus 2:1 says:

"AND THERE WENT A MAN OF THE HOUSE OF LEVI, AND TOOK TO WIFE A DAUGHTER OF LEVI."

Amram did not go into an ordinary house or family to take a wife. Instead he took a wife out of a priestly (Levi) home. He did not want to be unequally yoked with a woman who was not from a home of a priest or a pastor. He wanted a wife and a mother of his children. No, he was not looking for a girlfriend or any woman for a wife. Certainly, the young lady prepared and kept herself for her husband. As a Levi, he knew her, and she bore him sons according to Exodus 6:20:

"AND AMRAM TOOK HIM JOCHEBED HIS FATHER'S SISTER TO WIFE; AND SHE BARE HIM AARON AND MOSES: AND THE YEARS OF THE LIFE OF AMRAM WERE AN HUNDRED AND THIRTY AND SEVEN YEARS."

The traditions and customs at the time allowed him to marry his father's sister, his aunt, if you please. In his commentary, this is what Matthew Henry says about intermarriage between the tribe of Levi and Judah:

*"For the tribes of Levi and Judah often intermarried. It must not be omitted that Moses has recorded the marriage*

*of his father Amram with Jochebed his own aunt and it appears by Numbers 26:59 that it must be taken strictly for his father's own sister, at least by the half blood. This marriage was afterwards forbidden as incestuous (Leviticus 18:12), which might be looked upon as a blot upon his family, though before that law; yet Moses does not conceal it, for he sought not his own praise, but wrote with a sincere regard to truth, whether it smiled or frowned upon him. He concludes it with a particular mark of honor on the persons he is writing of, though he himself was one of them, Exodus 6:26, 27. These are that Moses and Aaron whom God pitched upon to be his plenipotentiaries in this treaty. These were those to whom God spoke (Exodus 6:26), and who spoke to Pharaoh on Israel's behalf, Exodus 6:27. Note, communion with God and serviceableness to his church are things that, above any other, put true honor upon men. Those are great indeed with whom God converses and whom he employs on his service. Such were that Moses and Aaron; and something of this honor have all his saints, who are made to our God kings and priests."*

Look at what God did with Jochebed's life and her son, Moses. Although she married her brother's son, Amram, God honored this union and blessed them with three children. Moses the third child and the second boy was used in a mighty way by God; he brought the children of Israel out of Egypt. Aaron was the high priest and

Moses' interpreter, and Miriam, was a prophetess, in whose merits the children of Israel had water during the 40years wandering in the desert. In all of the scriptures, Jochebed was the only one with three famous children. All of Jochebed's children were used of God in the liberation and the transition of Israel from Egypt to Yahweh promise land. God did this despite her seemingly unacceptable incestuous marital condition. This is the life and humble background of the mother of Moses, the great deliverer. It seems God's eternal purpose always, I mean, literally always supersedes man's sin, shortcomings or faults.

Woman, God will fulfill His eternal purpose for your life no matter what you do or don't do as long as you continue to trust in Him and His Grace to fulfill His eternal purposes for your life. God's acts, in the affairs of the earth and man, are eternally influenced by His divine and eternal purpose, not man's happiness.

## JOCHEBED'S FAITH

What made Jochebed different? What made her an extraordinary woman? Is it because of the child Moses? Certainly not! Exodus 2:2 revealed to us why she is considered an extraordinary and remarkable woman. It wasn't because she was born unto a priest nor because she was a Jewess. We know of many women born unto Christian parents or who are referred to as pastor's kids

UNLEASHING THE MOTHER IN YOU

but have no practicing or active faith in God. Moses writes in Exodus, chapter two:

"AND THE WOMAN CONCEIVED, AND BARE A SON: AND WHEN SHE SAW HIM THAT HE WAS A GOODLY CHILD, SHE HID HIM THREE MONTHS. AND WHEN SHE COULD NO LONGER HIDE HIM, SHE TOOK FOR HIM AN ARK OF BULRUSHES, AND DAUBED IT WITH SLIME AND WITH PITCH, AND PUT THE CHILD THEREIN; AND SHE LAID IT IN THE FLAGS BY THE RIVER'S BRINK." EXODUS 2:2

Jochebed was no ordinary woman in the scripture. She is revealed in the text as a woman of faith for the most part by her journey (works) because faith without works is dead. James says, "Show me your faith and I show you my faith by my works." James 2:14-26. Indeed faith without works is dead. The faith of Jochebed, just like any believer's faith, was put to the test by the decree of the King of Egypt, The Pharaoh. It was a death sentence passed in chapter one of the book of Exodus to kill every male child of the Hebrew women. It is a chilling and devilish decision ordered simply because God blessed Israel and the people of God became very great. It will be helpful if we take a closer look at the scriptural text:

"AND THE KING OF EGYPT SPAKE TO THE HEBREW MIDWIVES, OF WHICH THE NAME OF THE ONE WAS SHIPHRAH, AND THE NAME OF THE OTHER

PUAH: AND HE SAID, WHEN YE DO THE OFFICE OF A MIDWIFE TO THE HEBREW WOMEN, AND SEE THEM UPON THE STOOLS; IF IT BE A SON, THEN YE SHALL KILL HIM: BUT IF IT BE A DAUGHTER, THEN SHE SHALL LIVE." EXODUS 1:15-16

The seventh verse of Exodus chapter one gives the background of the King's decree. The Egyptians' leader and certainly the nation became fearful of the Israelites. The verse says emphatically that Israel became fruitful, and increased abundantly and multiplied, and waxed exceeding mighty." It doesn't end there, but it goes on to say and it gets better, **"And the land was filled with them."** You talk about God's blessings, this is a perfect picture. They were refugees, yet they were so blessed that the host nation, Egypt and its king became fearful of them because of the blessings of God.

As a woman of God, whether you have given birth to a child or not, you are blessed. The blessings of God upon your life are yet to manifest. The manifestation of the blessings of God according to Exodus 1:7 occurred in five dimensions. This is the fivefold manifestation of the blessings of Jehovah. They were fruitful, they increased abundantly, they multiplied, they waxed exceedingly mighty, and they occupied the land fully.

Jochebed is one of many Israelite women who had given birth to children in the land. She had Aaron and Miriam already. She had seen or heard or at the least, read about the blessings of God upon the Hebrews, her people. They had increased from seventy-five to literally millions. As one born in the house of Levi, she is aware of God's covenant with Abraham, Isaac, and Jacob. She is living in the moment of the manifestation of the blessings of the covenant. Though in a foreign land, and far away from destiny, she is a witness of God's blessings on her people. They are bearing fruit under difficult conditions and had increased abundantly in every imaginable dimension. They had multiplied in number and were militarily mightier than the Egyptians. Besides, they could be found in every part of the land of Egypt. This became fearful and dreadful to the Egyptians.

It was at this peak of the blessings of God that the King of Egypt gave his diabolical command to the midwives assigned to the Hebrew women to kill the male children. Certainly this attack on the boys was an attack against men and the future continuity of the nation. However, it is at this time that Jochebed was pregnant with Moses, the deliverer of Israel from Egypt. She was not afraid of the King's command nor was she stressed out. Her faith in God propelled her to act. That is what true faith in God does. It is always followed by a divine act that attracts the intervention of God. Jochebed's faith was seen in her response to Pharaoh's threat to kill her son, the deliverer of Israel.

In Exodus 2:2, Jochebed conceived, and bare a son and when she saw that he was a goodly child, she hid him three months. She acted in response to the King's threat, but out of faith instead of fear. God always responds to our faith and not to fear. God honored her act of faith when she singlehandedly hid him in her home for three months. That means, for three months, baby Moses was secured as a treasure or stored up in their home in such a way that the authorities were unaware of the presence of a male child. They could not take him away or kill him because God protected him in response to her faith in God.

Now, that is faith in action. Truly, God is a rewarder of those who diligently seek Him. Jochebed sought God for the protection of her life for violating the King's command, but more so, she sought God for the preservation of Moses' life. And for three months he was saved from the hands of the enemy. By faith, Jochebed treasured Moses. Little did she know that God had a plan for her baby boy.

If you will see and experience the hand of God supernaturally, you have to trust him completely. That trust has to be demonstrated by your acts of obedience to God than in fear of man and his threats. The next verse says that when she could no longer hide him in their home, she acted again and God honored her faith and obedience to Him. She made for Moses, an ark that she daubed with slime and with pitch. She placed her son in the ark and placed it in the river. This was not sensible nor was it wise, but an act of faith, generated by confidence and trust in God and is solely anchored in the living God, which does not always make sense nor does it appeal to the prudent of this age. What Jochebed did to secure her son, many women would not have done under the given circumstances. But this woman of faith understood that faith in God must be demonstrated by action that will make a demand on God to respond supernaturally. You, as a woman of God can operate in faith instead of fear.

When we consider the outcome and the result of her faith, we know without a doubt that God's hand was providentially upon Jochebed, Moses' mother. However, because God had marked Moses to deliver Israel from Egypt, God honored the demonstration of her faith by making sure the boy was secured, adopted into the royal family, educated in the best schools in Egypt, and fulfilled his God-given mission, the deliverance of Israel from Egyptian bondage.

## FAITH HAS ITS REWARD

In the book of Hebrews 11:1, 2 we read the definition of faith and the reward of faith. During the course of the writing of this book, God showed me the simplicity of faith and its outcome. Hebrews 11:1 defines faith, while verse 2 challenges the believer to demonstrate or exercise faith in God.

"NOW FAITH IS THE SUBSTANCE OF THINGS HOPED FOR, THE EVIDENCE OF THINGS NOT SEEN. FOR BY IT THE ELDERS OBTAINED A GOOD REPORT." HEBREWS 11:1-2

The second verse says, by faith, the elders obtained a good report. You obtain a good report when your faith is exercised in God's ability and power to manifest results when He is pleased by your faith. What He does as a result of your believing is the good report. For example, the security when Moses mother hid him for three months is the good report or testimony that she obtained, because that is what she believed God would do for her. God rewards the faith of the faithful. So the reward of faith or believing is God's response to your believing. The miracle is the good report you obtain when you trust God to show up and come through for you.

Remember what God told Abram in Genesis 15. After He called Abram in chapter 12, God appeared to him and made a covenant with him in chapter 15. *"I am thy shield and thy exceeding great reward."* God announced himself to Abram as his reward if he would trust and rely upon Him. In this case, Abram needed a seed, a child who would be born to him and carry his name. Whatever we are in need of or whatever our needs are when we seek Him, God provides, He meets us at the point of our need, and gives Himself, as the reward. He was Abram's reward. That is why He is the all sufficient God. Today, "God is a rewarder of those who diligently seek Him." Practically, when we are exercising faith in God for something, we are seeking Him and His intervention in the situation, like Abram did in Gen.15. It will be very helpful if we read the text.

"AFTER THESE THINGS THE WORD OF THE LORD CAME TO ABRAM IN A VISION SAYING, "DO NOT BE AFRAID, ABRAM, I AM YOUR SHIELD, YOUR EXCEEDING GREAT REWARD." (GENESIS 15:1-2)

God revealed to me during my meditation that those who diligently seek Him first experience his presence, and in some cases, His glory first before He gives them the tangibles. He gives Himself to us first, and then he gives us what we need. God showed me that it is His presence and power that manifests primarily in our lives and circumstances before the things we need or want. It is His presence that leads us and guides us along the way. God is our sufficiency.

Now, let us examine how Jochebed's faith was rewarded by God's presence and how He supernaturally provided what she needed. First she conceived and gave birth to Moses at the time when the King of Egypt passed a decree for all male children of the Hebrew women to be killed by the midwives during childbirth. Secondly, she hid her son after birth for three months and God protected both of them until it became unsafe for the child. Thirdly, God's presence with the child secured him and gave him favor when Pharaoh's daughter opened the ark and saw him. God protected Moses and provided him an adopted mother, and he became Pharaoh's daughter's son. Fourthly, God rewarded her faith when she became the Hebrew nurse for her own son. How was all of this possible? Jochebed's faith in a God who is our exceeding and great reward.

## JOCHEBED'S MISSION

After the birth of Moses, Jochebed understood her mission. Her success, just like any other Christian was to fulfill that mission. The late Russ Tatro always defined success as "Knowing the will of God and doing it." You are not successful simply because you know the will of God for your life. It is doing His will and fulfilling it. Most Christians define success by what they possess materially or financially. It is committing our lives to God's plan. God's plan is the mission or assignment he gives you and me to accomplish. Making the mission a reality or fulfilling the mission becomes your purpose for living.

All of a sudden, your life is defined by your purpose in life. You laugh and love, sit and stand, sing and shout, and breath and live, to accomplish your purpose, which is His plan, and His mission. God's plan must become your purpose.

While on a retreat recently, I grabbed a June 2011 Ebony magazine and read a very interesting article about De Von Franklin, the vice president for Columbia pictures, a Christian minister and a motivational speaker. In the book *Enjoy Real Success without Losing Your True Self*, this is what he said:

"When we commit ourselves to God, we understand that He has plans for us. You do not have to compromise who you are. And I want God's will in my life more than I want position. And so I believe that in pursuing His will and pursuing my purpose, position and promotion will come. Not everybody can play the game the way others play it, because that might not be organic as you are and who God has made you. So part of thinking outside the box is being completely open to how God wants to work specifically and uniquely in your life and career."

This is a profound truth. Jochebed certainly demonstrated commitment to God and understood God's plan for her life as a woman. Her "calling" was to conceive, give birth, mother, and protect Moses, Israel's Deliverer. She knew her purpose, and she pursued it violently. She knew

God's will for her life and I believe that she understood and committed her life to fulfilling her mission. This is evident in the outcome. Moses became the man God intended for him to become because of a persistent and wise mother.

Jochebed took good care of little Moses. And I believe that she told him who he was and the stories of how he became Pharaoh's daughters' son. She instilled in him the virtues she possessed and taught him to be brave and risk his life to save his brethren just as she and Miriam had done. Moses grew up to be the greatest man that ever lived. He knew where he came from and who he was in Christ that is why he risked his life to save a fellow-Jew from a cruel slave-driver and eventually delivered the children of Israel from the Egyptians and into the Promised Land.

Jochebed was considered the mother of 600,000 children because she gave birth to Moses who was worth as much as all the people of Israel that came out of Egypt.

Jochebed also raised an amazing, godly woman, Miriam, who also lead all the Jewish women and walked in the office of the prophetic. She also raised Aaron who received the crown of priesthood. What an amazing woman of God! My prayer is that we all can learn from Jochebed as we raise godly children.

Imagine for a second the pain Jochebed felt after Moses

was weaned and she had to give him up once again. She had to bring her precious child and give him to the Pharoah's daughter. How that must have torn her mother's heart to have her son returned to her only to give him up forever a few years later. She must have wondered why; she must have ached years afterward for her son, yet she was unable to hold him.

The Bible does not tell us what happened to Jochebed after that. There was no account of her seeing her son Moses again. Perhaps she lived to see the glorious day of freedom for her people. Perhaps she eventually understood why she had to go through the pain of letting Moses go. However, more than likely, she died in Egypt. After all, it would be eighty years before God would use her son to accomplish His plan in freeing His people. She may have died in slavery wondering what had happened to the son she had lost.

She did not know what would be the end, but she did her part. She didn't know why God would have her go through all of the pain, but she let her son go. How many of us would willingly do that? We all too often want to know the reasons why we have to suffer as we do. We want to know what the future will be. However, like Jochebed, we must surrender. We must let go of our hopes, our dreams ... our "rights." We must leave them in God's hands and trust Him to work the details out.

He does indeed have a plan. We must follow Him even when it sounds crazy.

As a woman you should always remember the example of Jochebed, and like her, purpose to follow God wherever He leads and do whatever He says. God will indeed work all His little details out if we simply trust. Once you identify your God-given mission and use every God-given resource to accomplish that mission, you are living for your purpose. Do not compromise it for anything promised by man, promotion, position or fame. After you have done the will of God, you will obtain the promise and a good report or testimony.

## MIRIAM: THE BABYSITTER

Moses writes as he was told in Exodus two verse four. His sister Miriam watched her mother as she placed her brother in the ark and perhaps asked her to watch what would happen to him. This is what the verse says:

AND HIS SISTER [MIRIAM] STOOD SOME DISTANCE AWAY TO [B] LEARN WHAT WOULD BE DONE TO HIM. EXODUS 2:4

Miriam was aware of the evil times surrounding the birth of her brother Moses — the death threats of all male children born to the Hebrew women. She probably witnessed her parents' frustration when they could no

45

longer hide Moses. She also may have witnessed the episode when the authorities had come to search for hidden babies. When it became apparent that they could no longer hide Moses with the cruel decree of the King of Egypt, she stood afar watching to see what would become of her brother. I like to think of Miriam's role as a babysitter or watcher for her mother.

Miriam was not the biological mother of Moses, yet as a woman, no doubt she demonstrated, by her actions, the qualities of a mother. Our purpose is to portray Miriam as a mother, though she is Moses' sister, yet through her, we encourage every woman reading this book to see herself not just as a woman, but as a mother. Whatever the circumstances or reasons why you have not given birth to your own children, you are naturally a mother. The mother in you is not determined or visible only when you give birth. You are limiting the God-given mothering abilities in you when you display the mother in you only for your biological child. When you can be trusted to take care of somebody else's child then God will give you yours. This is a principal of stewardship.

When you care for a child without a parent or support or adopt an orphan, you activate the grace and mercy of God to manifest His power and to bring you the miracle that you need. I have witnessed the results of God's power causing women to conceive and give birth to their own children after they activated the power of God by their faith in action. Our society's views of women who have not given birth to children also affects most women's ability to mother. Given that Miriam is responding as a sister to Moses, yet it was the mother in her that took action. I am convinced that in every woman is a mother.

## MIRIAM'S ROLE

Miriam's family must have known the schedule of the Pharaoh's daughter; or maybe not, but providence may have prevailed. I believe they knew the days and the time of the day she came down from her royal residence to bathe in the river. Better still, what is even more powerful is the truth that Jochebed may have received directions from God to build the ark for the protection of the child and his release upon the river. Whatever the case, Miriam was ready to play the role of a mother in Moses' life at this time. At different points of everyone's life, somebody, man or woman, babysat you. In Moses' case, different women mothered him in his journey to becoming the deliverer of Israel.

Babysitters are those who take care of or look after babies or children in the absence of the parents. So if Miriam is looking after Moses, being placed by the banks of the river, as an act of faith on the part of Jochebed, there must be a caregiver or caretaker to watch over him and observe what would happen to him. After all that is what babysitters do. They provide services that the child needs in the absence of the parents. Feeding, changing, protecting, rocking to sleep, to name a few, are some of the basic services babysitters provide for children under their care. When a caregiver or babysitter provides the needs of a child in the absence of the mother, that woman is mothering that child in that sense. Miriam, as a big sister, mothers Moses during the period he is in the ark upon the river leading up to the moment Pharaoh's daughter adopted him.

## MIRIAM THE PROPHETESS

Miriam was with her brother through the exodus from Egypt and was with him throughout the nine plagues. She was a woman of God. She was indeed a prophet herself (Exodus 15:20). She was called to play a less prominent role than Moses but nevertheless a vital one. As a woman, you should never despise your role in the ministry. It may be less prominent than that of your husband; nevertheless it is a role God has chosen for you. The mother of Moses fulfilled her destiny. She brought up a godly child. Jochebed, Moses' mother (Numbers 26:59, Exodus 6:20) is not well-known yet she played one of the most important roles in the nation of Israel and indeed the Church.

Miriam played an important role as well, and the Bible recorded her as the first woman to lead a choir (the women of Israel) as they crossed the Red Sea.

Dear Woman, maybe God has called you to serve as an usher, as a childcare minister, in the youth ministry or in a small group within your church. Maybe you are an encourager, intercessor or exhorter and have used these gifts to minister to several people in a way that does not seem very significant. Or maybe you are presently bringing up children, like the mother of Moses, or babysitting other people's children like Miriam; do not consider your job as insignificant. God rewards and blesses us for being faithful in the things He has called us to do and not in the things we want to do. Contentment with our calling in life is vital if we are to avoid growing envious of others.

Miriam was envious of Moses and criticized his choice for a wife and God punished her for it. God's judgment on Miriam was swift and severe (Numbers 12).

If you have a husband who God is using make sure you honor and respect the gift and anointing on his life despite his weaknesses. We always need to honor the people of God. Rather than accepting her place in God's plan and serving with gladness, Miriam allowed herself to be overcome by feelings of resentment.

Praise God for women like Miriam, who although she fell into sin, rose again to declare God's wondrous works.

We must keep looking up, being grateful, and desiring to be used of God not to be noticed, but so when we stand before God we can hear Him clearly and can be used like Miriam.

# THE MIDWIVES CRISIS: THE DELIVERERS OF MOSES

The Hebrews (Israel) became a powerful nation in Egypt because of the blessings of God upon them. Though they were in a foreign land as slaves, yet God was faithful in providing, protecting, increasing, and multiplying them to the extent of making their presence visible in every part of the land of Egypt. They became mightier and powerful than Egypt.

## SLAVERY AND SUFFERING OF ISRAEL

As though the slavery, bondage, suffering, and inhumane treatment of the Jews were not enough, the King of Egypt, who did not know Joseph and the history of his influence and leadership in Egypt during the reign of his predecessor, passed a decree to kill every male child. His decision was clearly out of fear and his purpose and intention was to slow, weaken or stop the growth and might of Israel. The text below not only reveals the fear, intimidation, threat and insecurity the Jews posed for the new king and his nation but also reveals how they afflicted God's people, his plan to kill all the baby boys, and how God used ordinary women, the two midwives, Shiphrah and Puah to save the Hebrew boys, including Moses.

"NOW THERE AROSE UP A NEW KING OVER EGYPT, WHICH KNEW NOT JOSEPH. AND HE SAID UNTO HIS PEOPLE, BEHOLD, THE PEOPLE OF THE CHILDREN OF ISRAEL ARE MORE AND MIGHTIER THAN WE: COME ON, LET US DEAL WISELY WITH THEM; LEST THEY MULTIPLY, AND IT COME TO PASS, THAT, WHEN THERE FALLETH OUT ANY WAR, THEY JOIN ALSO UNTO OUR ENEMIES, AND FIGHT AGAINST US, AND SO GET THEM UP OUT OF THE LAND. THEREFORE THEY DID SET OVER THEM TASKMASTERS TO AFFLICT THEM WITH THEIR BURDENS. AND THEY BUILT FOR PHARAOH TREASURE CITIES, PITHOM AND RAAMSES. BUT THE MORE THEY AFFLICTED THEM, THE MORE THEY MULTIPLIED AND GREW. AND THEY WERE GRIEVED BECAUSE OF THE CHILDREN OF ISRAEL. AND THE EGYPTIANS MADE THE CHILDREN OF ISRAEL TO SERVE WITH RIGOR: AND THEY MADE THEIR LIVES BITTER WITH HARD BONDAGE, IN MORTAR, AND IN BRICK, AND IN ALL MANNER OF SERVICE IN THE FIELD: ALL THEIR SERVICE, WHEREIN THEY MADE THEM SERVE, WAS WITH RIGOR. AND THE KING OF EGYPT SPAKE TO THE HEBREW MIDWIVES, OF WHICH THE NAME OF THE ONE WAS SHIPHRAH,

AND THE NAME OF THE OTHER PUAH: AND HE SAID, WHEN YE DO THE OFFICE OF A MIDWIFE TO THE HEBREW WOMEN, AND SEE THEM UPON THE STOOLS; IF IT BE A SON, THEN YE SHALL KILL HIM: BUT IF IT BE A DAUGHTER, THEN SHE SHALL LIVE. BUT THE MIDWIVES FEARED GOD, AND DID NOT AS THE KING OF EGYPT COMMANDED THEM, BUT SAVED THE MEN CHILDREN ALIVE. AND THE KING OF EGYPT CALLED FOR THE MIDWIVES, AND SAID UNTO THEM, WHY HAVE YE DONE THIS THING, AND HAVE SAVED THE MEN CHILDREN ALIVE? AND THE MIDWIVES SAID UNTO PHARAOH, BECAUSE THE HEBREW WOMEN ARE NOT AS THE EGYPTIAN WOMEN; FOR THEY ARE LIVELY, AND ARE DELIVERED ERE THE MIDWIVES COME IN UNTO THEM. THEREFORE GOD DEALT WELL WITH THE MIDWIVES: AND THE PEOPLE MULTIPLIED, AND WAXED VERY MIGHTY. AND IT CAME TO PASS, BECAUSE THE MIDWIVES FEARED GOD, THAT HE MADE THEM HOUSES. AND PHARAOH CHARGED ALL HIS PEOPLE, SAYING, "EVERY SON THAT IS BORN YE SHALL CAST INTO THE RIVER, AND EVERY DAUGHTER YE SHALL SAVE ALIVE." EXODUS 1:8-22

## PHARAOH'S EVIL COMMAND

AND THE KING OF EGYPT SPAKE TO THE HEBREW MIDWIVES, OF WHICH THE NAME OF THE ONE WAS SHIPHRAH, AND THE NAME OF THE OTHER PUAH: AND HE SAID, "WHEN YE DO THE OFFICE

OF A MIDWIFE TO THE HEBREW WOMEN, AND SEE
THEM UPON THE STOOLS; IF IT BE A SON, THEN YE
SHALL KILL HIM: BUT IF IT BE A DAUGHTER, THEN
SHE SHALL LIVE." EXODUS 1:15-16

Pharaoh's plan and strategy is clearly revealed in the text above. He actually spoke to the midwives face-to-face and ordered them to kill all the sons born to Hebrew women under their care. They were ordered to murder the boys as soon as they were recognized at birth. This cold blooded killing of the male children was designed to eliminate the nation of Israel and destroy their military might and capability, and at the same time make the women venerable perhaps to servitude and hopelessness.

The description of the setting and timing of the murder of the boys is evident. It was during the birthing process, while the Hebrew women were still on the birthing stool or birthing table of the midwives that the heartless murder of the boys was to take place. No boy child was given the right to live. The King's decree took away each child's life before he actually inhaled his first breath. How did God deliver Moses from the death decree of Pharaoh? Exodus 1:17-18 reveals that God used Egyptian women who were the midwives assigned to attend to the Hebrew women while giving birth.

BUT THE MIDWIVES FEARED GOD, AND DID NOT
AS THE KING OF EGYPT COMMANDED THEM, BUT

SAVED THE MEN CHILDREN ALIVE. AND THE KING OF EGYPT CALLED FOR THE MIDWIVES, AND SAID UNTO THEM, WHY HAVE YE DONE THIS THING, AND HAVE SAVED THE MEN CHILDREN ALIVE? AND THE MIDWIVES SAID UNTO PHARAOH, BECAUSE THE HEBREW WOMEN ARE NOT AS THE EGYPTIAN WOMEN; FOR THEY ARE LIVELY, AND ARE DELIVERED ERE THE MIDWIVES COME IN UNTO THEM. EXODUS 1:17-19

## THE FEAR OF GOD

The fear of God came upon the midwives instead of the fear of the king. This is the only reason why the midwives could not and did not obey the command of the king of Egypt, but saved the children. They feared God over the king of Egypt, who was just another man. When we fear God, He gives us wisdom. These ordinary women and midwives became extraordinary women when they played the role of mothers in Moses' life at birth. They exercised the bravery and the heroism that is innate in every woman and delivered Moses from death. They did this at their own peril. In their fear for God, they exercised their faith in the power and ability of God to save and deliver them from the wicked king of Egypt.

The text says, "They saved the male children alive," that tells us that there were other boys they saved besides Moses. Moses' deliverance is recorded in scriptures because the plan of God for his life was tied to the plan of God for the deliverance of Israel. Israel's destiny was tied to Moses' and the destiny of the midwives was tied to Moses and Israel, therefore their performance of their mission as mothers in his life was critical at his birth. Their willingness to obey God, despite the death penalty, distinguished them from all other midwives in the land and moved God to first bless them with wisdom to answer the King why the boys were increasing in the land. And they answered the King saying,

"THE HEBREW WOMEN ARE AS THE EGYPTIAN WOMEN; FOR THEY ARE LIVELY, AND ARE DELIVERED ERE THE MIDWIVES COME IN UNTO THEM."

When God is at work, and he is working in and through you, you may be known as a weaker vessel, an ignorant or uneducated woman, but because it is God, who is working out His purpose in you and through you, you will cease to be a weaker, ignorant or uneducated woman. As a vessel or woman in the hand of God becomes an instrument in the hand of God to destroy the works and plans of the devil and his agents and at the same time, fulfill His purpose. So shall God use you. And when this happens, you do cease to be ordinary and become extraordinary because of the manifestation of the supernatural power and wisdom of God.

The testimony of the midwives to the king of Egypt about the Hebrew women is no doubt the testimony of God's supernatural power at work when they gave birth during this dark chapter of their history in Egypt. Before the midwives came, the women gave birth to the male children. Their own decision not to obey the King's edict to kill all male children, but save them alive was also the supernatural workings of God. This also is the gift of faith at work in these midwives. For them to save the male children alive, against the order of their king, was an act of no ordinary faith but the gift of faith to disobey the king, believing that God would deliver them from death as well. They were on a mission to deliver the deliverer of Israel and when they acted in faith, they allowed the mothering qualities in them to come out to protect and save Moses from death in the River Nile, according to the command of the king.

## GOD'S DEALINGS WITH THE MIDWIVES

THEREFORE GOD DEALT WELL WITH THE MIDWIVES: AND THE PEOPLE MULTIPLIED, AND WAXED VERY MIGHTY. AND IT CAME TO PASS, BECAUSE THE MIDWIVES FEARED GOD, THAT HE MADE THEM HOUSES. AND PHARAOH CHARGED ALL HIS PEOPLE, SAYING, "EVERY SON THAT IS BORN YE SHALL CAST INTO THE RIVER, AND EVERY DAUGHTER YE SHALL SAVE ALIVE." EXODUS 1:20-22

We believe that the Egyptian midwives' fear for the God of Israel made them willing and ready to obey God. The fear of the Lord is the beginning of wisdom. That means, when you fear the Lord, He will give or impact His wisdom to you. Think about the magnitude of the consequences of their decision to save the boys alive instead of drowning them in the River Nile. This was also a strong operation of the wisdom of God. The decision not to kill the male children by drowning was the wisdom of God. It would have been easier to drown the boys, but they chose the hardest decision, to go against the king's order, to kill every boy child.

So how did God deal with the midwives? The answer is twofold. *"The people multiplied and waxed very mighty and God made them houses."* It is obvious that as the midwives honored God, Israel continued to increase, multiply, and grow mightily; evidenced as the boys matured into manhood, married, and multiplied, causing the nation to increase in number and fill every portion of the land of Egypt. This growth and multiplication also contributed to the military might of Israel. This military power was God's protection for the midwives. Their actions in saving the male children gave them and the Jews a sense of security. Secondly, God gave them houses. They were both protected and provided houses or homes for their families because the Lord remembered them for their motherly role as deliverers or defenders of the male children.

How is this applicable to you as a woman? As a woman, what is your mission in life? The midwives knew their mission in life and that they did to the pleasing and the glory of God. They knew that God's mission for them was to save lives. Guess what, they saved the lives of the male children of the very Hebrew women whose sons Pharaoh had ordered to be drowned in the river. This is how you will know the mission of God, when you joyfully obey God's Word in the face of death, ridicule, disgrace, and misinterpretation of your actions. These midwives' actions put them in a position of honor and blessings that elevated them to a new level in God and in the eyes of the Jews. Every Hebrew woman whose male child they delivered remembered and blessed them. Besides, God Almighty took note and blessed them physically and materially.

Usually, your mission in life as an individual or as a woman is often discovered in your line of work, which in most cases is as a result of your passion in life. As midwives or nurses, these women's mission in life was to deliver babies and keep them alive. As they sought to fulfill that mission, they became passionate about saving the male children of the Hebrew slaves despite the threat of the Pharaoh. The mothering abilities and instincts surfaced passionately for the deliverance of Moses and the other male children that they saved alive. Shiphrah and Puah served as Moses' mothers as they fulfilled their mission at his birth. They saved him and the other male children alive. You can mother a child or be a mother in a child's life whether or not he or she is your biological child. The choice is yours to act when the opportunity presents itself to you.

## PHARAOH'S DAUGHTER: MOSES ADOPTED MOTHER

Indeed, God moves in mysterious ways. He moves in ways that we do not understand partly because of the things He allows or permits in the process in order to accomplish His purpose for you as a woman. The daughter of Pharaoh, the king of Egypt, is pulled in the circle of women who have been chosen and positioned by God to mother Moses after his biological mother placed him in the ark and upon the River Nile. The king passed the decree to kill all male children at birth and to drown the baby boys in the River Nile, yet in the plan of God it is his daughter who will see Moses on the river, save, and adopt him as her own.

His daughter found Moses in the ark on the River Nile and instead of drowning Moses, God intervened supernaturally as his sister Miriam is following and watching to see what would happen to him while his mother was praying for the safety of her son.

Thank God for the king's decree because it impacted the mother of Moses in at least two ways. First, she became a better person by becoming a woman of faith, as she trusted God for her son's safety. Faith in God makes you a better person. Faith, which is the sixth sense of the believer, makes all things possible for the believing woman of God. And God answered her. Secondly, she became creative and innovative because she built the first boat or ship and placed Moses in it to float on the River Nile when it became apparent that she and her husband could not protect him on land and at home. If she did not have the pressure of the threat of her son's death, the creativity in her would have never surfaced. God had a plan to take Moses into the King's palace. The pressure brought the best out of her.

## DIVINE DECREE SUPERSEDES MAN'S DECREE

The scripture below revealed that in the midst of the uncertain future of the deliverer of Israel, Moses, as he floated on the River Nile due to the king's decree, God's decree executed through his daughter, saved the child's life, preserved him, and adopted him as her son, thus making him the Pharaoh's grandson.

AND THE DAUGHTER OF PHARAOH CAME DOWN TO WASH HERSELF AT THE RIVER; AND HER MAIDENS WALKED ALONG BY THE RIVER'S SIDE; AND WHEN SHE SAW THE ARK AMONG THE FLAGS, SHE SENT HER MAID TO FETCH IT. AND WHEN SHE HAD OPENED IT, SHE SAW THE CHILD: AND, BEHOLD, THE BABE WEPT. AND SHE HAD COMPASSION ON HIM, AND SAID, THIS IS ONE OF THE HEBREW'S CHILDREN. THEN SAID HIS SISTER TO PHARAOH'S DAUGHTER, SHALL I GO AND CALL TO THEE A NURSE OF THE HEBREW WOMEN, THAT SHE MAY NURSE THE CHILD FOR THEE? AND PHARAOH'S DAUGHTER SAID TO HER, GO. AND THE MAID WENT AND CALLED THE CHILD'S MOTHER. AND PHARAOH'S DAUGHTER SAID UNTO HER, TAKE THIS CHILD AWAY, AND NURSE IT FOR ME, AND I WILL GIVE THEE THY WAGES. AND THE WOMAN TOOK THE CHILD, AND NURSED IT. AND THE CHILD GREW, AND SHE BROUGHT HIM UNTO PHARAOH'S DAUGHTER, AND HE BECAME HER SON. AND SHE CALLED HIS NAME MOSES: AND SHE SAID, BECAUSE I DREW HIM OUT OF THE WATER. EXODUS 2:5-10

When it looked like all hell had broken loose, her son's life was unsafe, and death was inevitable due to the Pharaoh's decree, God's decree superseded his decree. A number of tiny yet orderly and divine events unfolded. Our text says, the daughter of Pharaoh came down to wash herself at the river. God moved her to come down by divine timing; to attend to the baby in the ark floating on the river. The mother of Moses by divine leading placed him on the river so that the Pharaoh's daughter would meet him on schedule and draw him out of the river. Secondly, she noticed the ark among the river plants. Thank God He made her see the ark. Thirdly, she commanded her maid to bring the ark and as she opened the ark, the baby began to cry. She had compassion on him and identified him as a child of a Hebrew.

This was no coincidence, but the act of God to fulfill His divine purpose for Moses' life. It was God working all things together for the good of Moses, his mother, Miriam, Pharaoh's daughter, and Israel. Most importantly, God worked it out for His glory because each one was called to fulfill his purpose. Whatever God calls you to accomplish in the life of a child, and it could be anything small or great, significant or insignificant, according to man's standard, it is always to fulfill his divine and eternal purpose. Just do it. And as you do, you fulfill divine purpose.

Pharaoh's daughter in the end received Moses back from his biological mother according to the agreement to nurse him for wages. His mother brought him back after he grew. When the biological mother brought him back, notice that the text says, "He became her son." He became the son of Pharaoh's daughter by adoption. She adopted Moses as her son to fulfill the purpose of God. "Adoption" was the means that God used to preserve Moses in the king's palace in order to deliver Israel from the bondage and slavery of Egypt. When she adopted him, she called him Moses because she drew him out of the water.

## THE MAN, MOSES

"AND IT CAME TO PASS IN THOSE DAYS, WHEN MOSES WAS GROWN, THAT HE WENT OUT UNTO HIS BRETHREN, AND LOOKED ON THEIR BURDENS: AND HE SPIED AN EGYPTIAN SMITING AN HEBREW, ONE OF HIS BRETHREN. AND HE LOOKED THIS WAY AND THAT WAY AND WHEN HE SAW THAT THERE WAS NO MAN, HE SLEW THE EGYPTIAN, AND HID HIM IN THE SAND." EXODUS 2:11

When Moses turned into a man, he became aware of his identity. Though he was educated in the culture and obtained the best education of Egypt, while living in the palace, he became aware that he was a Hebrew and not an Egyptian. What began as a dreadful, hopeless, and a dark ordeal for the Jews in Egypt, God spun different sizes and colors of threads to produce a beautiful story. He called together different women alongside his biological mother to nurture him when she could not provide the care, love, protection, and help he needed along his path to manhood.

God moves in mysterious ways indeed. He moves in ways that we do not understand partly because of the things He allows or permits in the process in order to accomplish His purpose. The daughter of Pharaoh is recognized as one of the women who have been chosen and positioned by God to mother Moses.

# CHAPTER 3
# MOTHER'S IMPACT DESTINIES

From all indications, the Egyptians made the Jews their enemies not so much because of what they did but because of what the Lord God did for His people. He blessed them and that blessing caused them to multiply and increase. The king of Egypt, the new Pharaoh, who did not know Joseph and the things he accomplished through his leadership, decided to antagonize God's people because he was afraid that Israel would turn against them in the event of war.

The new King's fear of the might of Israel led them to devise a demonic plan to minimize or reduce the growth of the nation as well as to oppress them spiritually and physically. They actually set task masters of the people of God who oppressed them by afflicting them with hard labor and the building of Pharaoh's treasure cities, Pithom and Raamses. It is at the peak of the execution of this evil plan that Pharaoh passed the cruel command saying,

"EVERY SON WHO IS BORN YOU SHALL CAST INTO

THE RIVER, AND EVERY DAUGHTER YOU SHALL SAVE ALIVE." EXODUS 1:22

Moses is born at this crucial and dark spot in the history of the Nation of Israel. There is no record in scripture that the Israelites obey this evil injunction of the King instead, God used the same river and the King's daughter to bring about His Divine Will. The River Nile was designated as the place for murder of every son who was born unto a Jewish family. Instead of drowning Moses, the Pharaoh daughter commanded that the child be brought to her when she found him floating on the river. The command was to drown him or kill him, but she asked for a maid to nurse him for a wage or salary. She had no idea that the maid, Jochebed, was Moses' mother. God used the very instrument designated to take the lives of baby boys to save Moses.

On the other hand, though her father passed the cruel and evil decree to have all the boys murdered in the Nile, God changed her heart when she saw Moses on the Nile. The Mother in her was released to save, care for, nurture, and adopt him as her own son and raise him right in the palace at the government of Egypt's expense. Wow, only God could have done this. As the scripture says in Proverbs,

"WHEN A MAN'S WAYS PLEASE THE LORD, HE

MAKETH EVEN HIS ENEMIES TO BE AT PEACE WITH HIM." PROVERBS 16:7

You see, I am convinced that the Pharaoh's daughter knew that Moses was a Hebrew, yet she realized that there was something different about this one, but there was nothing she could do about it. She also knew that keeping him alive against her father's command and taking the child into the palace was taking the enemy into the palace, but she could do nothing about it.

This is favor. This was an act of God when one's enemy is at peace him or her. God used the very River Nile to preserve Moses. Do not be afraid of that which has been set up to destroy you or your child. God will use it to work together for your good but for His Glory. Also, the Pharaoh's daughter became an instrument in the hand of God by divine favor upon the child to preserve his life. Instead of executing the judgment of death by her father's command, she executed God's plan of life, greatness, and leadership for Moses. This was God's Grace at work both to will and to do of His good pleasure to fulfill His purpose.

And lastly, God allowed the resources of Egypt to be used not just to pay Moses' mother for nursing her own son, but also to care for him from age three to manhood, including providing the best education and military training that Egypt had to offer Moses. Truly, God knows how to turn your bad situations around for the good of the faithful and those who trust Him.

# FROM THE PALACE INTO THE DESERT

Moses grew up in the King's Palace as the son of Pharaoh's daughter making him the Pharaoh's grandson. If everything had stayed the same, Moses probably would have become the next Pharaoh of Egypt. Moses becoming the son of the Pharaoh's daughter suggests one of two things. She probably could not have children or she did not have children as yet. This may have prompted the release of the mother in her to adopt him. As a prince and a grown up, he goes out to the fields one day and sees an evil done against one of his Hebrew brothers by an Egyptian. The episode that followed caused him to flee from the palace and the royalty he knew and enjoyed. This is what Exodus 2:11-15 says:

"AND IT CAME TO PASS IN THOSE DAYS, WHEN MOSES WAS GROWN, THAT HE WENT OUT UNTO HIS BRETHREN, AND LOOKED ON THEIR BURDENS: AND HE SPIED AN EGYPTIAN SMITING AN HEBREW, ONE OF HIS BRETHREN. AND HE LOOKED THIS WAY AND THAT WAY, AND WHEN HE SAW THAT THERE WAS NO MAN, HE SLEW THE EGYPTIAN, AND HID HIM IN THE SAND. AND WHEN HE WENT OUT THE

SECOND DAY, BEHOLD, TWO MEN OF THE HEBREWS STROVE TOGETHER: AND HE SAID TO HIM THAT DID THE WRONG, WHEREFORE SMITEST THOU THY FELLOW? AND HE SAID, WHO MADE THEE A PRINCE AND A JUDGE OVER US? INTENDS THOU TO KILL ME, AS THOU KILLST THE EGYPTIAN? AND MOSES FEARED, AND SAID, SURELY THIS THING IS KNOWN. NOW WHEN PHARAOH HEARD THIS THING, HE SOUGHT TO SLAY MOSES. BUT MOSES FLED FROM THE FACE OF PHARAOH, AND DWELT IN THE LAND OF MIDIAN: AND HE SAT DOWN BY A WELL."

What Moses thought was simple, became complicated. And what he thought was a secret became known to all including Pharaoh. It is apparent from the text that Moses became aware of the plight of his people, the Hebrews. So when he was grown, one- day he went out unto his brothers and sisters. He purposely went out to observe their burdens placed upon them by the taskmasters. I like to believe that Moses' motivation to visit with his people was prompted by his coming into alignment with the purpose of God for his life and for Israel. It was a decision to separate himself from the royalty of Egypt that was evil. The writer in the book of Hebrews had this to say about Moses.

"BY FAITH MOSES, WHEN HE WAS COME TO YEARS, REFUSED TO BE CALLED THE SON OF PHARAOH'S

DAUGHTER; CHOOSING RATHER TO SUFFER AFFLICTION WITH THE PEOPLE OF GOD, THAN TO ENJOY THE PLEASURES OF SIN FOR A SEASON." HEBREWS 11:24-25

It is clear that Moses made a conscious and informed decision to accept or refuse the throne of Egypt. The text above says he refused to be called the son of Pharaoh's daughter or by Pharaoh's name. He chose rather to suffer with the people of God. He identified with the oppressed Hebrews under the wicked slave masters of Egypt. His decision to kill the Egyptian who beat on one of his brothers reveals the evil that existed in and outside of the King's palace. His action also revealed his resolve to align himself with the plans and purposes of God at the expense of losing the fame, popularity, and the royalty he enjoyed as a prince or heir of the throne.

When it became clear to Moses that the word was out on him, he fled from Pharaoh's presence into the desert where he met with God and prepared for his ministry and mission in Egypt. Moses fled from Egypt and from the face of Pharaoh when he learned that Pharaoh sought to kill him. From all indications, it is clear that God allowed fearful and life threatening circumstances in his life to root him out of the palace into an unfamiliar environment in order fulfill His divine purpose and destiny. Furthermore, Josephus, the church historian said this about Moses.

"THE EGYPTIANS, FROM THE THRONE DOWN, WERE ENVIOUS OF MOSES, AND PARTLY AFRAID OF HIM. THEY THOUGHT, DUE TO HIS GREAT SUCCESSION DEFEATING THE ETHIOPIANS [THE JEWISH TARGUMS SAY THAT MOSES WAS A GENERAL IN THE EGYPTIAN ARMY], THAT HE MIGHT TAKE ADVANTAGE OF HIS GOOD FORTUNE AND TRY TO SUBVERT THEIR GOVERNMENT. SO WHEN MOSES, IN DEFENDING THE HEBREW KILLED AN EGYPTIAN, THIS WAS THE PROVERBIAL STRAW THAT BROKE THE CAMEL'S BACK."

Evidently, an event that began as an accident no doubt was supernaturally interwoven by God to simply usher Moses into his destiny, which included meeting his wife, his father in law, Jethro, and with the God of the Hebrews. It was while Moses tended to the flock of Jethro on the backside of the mountain that he saw a sight that intrigued him and ushered him into the presence of God.

## THE MEETING WITH GOD

Moses' meeting with God in the backside of the desert was designed by God so that He could personally tutor and equip Moses with divine spiritual instructions and grace to deliver Israel from the bondage of Pharaoh and Egypt. God orchestrated the events that caused Moses to flee from the face of Pharaoh because He wanted him to learn what he could not learn in the palace. The first three verses of Exodus chapter three clearly revealed the plot.

NOW MOSES KEPT THE FLOCK OF JETHRO HIS FATHER IN LAW, THE PRIEST OF MIDIAN: AND HE LED THE FLOCK TO THE BACKSIDE OF THE DESERT, AND CAME TO THE MOUNTAIN OF GOD, EVEN TO HOREB. AND THE ANGEL OF THE LORD APPEARED UNTO HIM IN A FLAME OF FIRE OUT OF THE MIDST OF A BUSH AND HE LOOKED, AND, BEHOLD, THE BUSH BURNED WITH FIRE, AND THE BUSH WAS NOT CONSUMED. EXODUS 3:1-3

The Lord appeared to Moses in a flame. He used the sight of the burning bush to attract and summon Moses to meet with Him. Truly, God uses the natural things to speak to us or teach us the spiritual. This marked the beginning of forty years of training that would break Moses, humble him and destroy dependence and hope in the wisdom and knowledge of Egypt and his personal skills and strength. God displayed His power personally, lending Moses the experiences that built up his faith in the power and the ability of God to deliver Israel. The personal revelations of God and the natural lessons for the development of his character, integrity, and faith in God, as he led the flock of Jethro, prepared and qualified him for the assignment to deliver Israel from Egypt. Thus, the message to Pharaoh "Let my people go" was and still is the purpose of God's calling upon the lives of ministers of the Gospel in our dispensation. After many generations, this truth, and principle still remains; the release of the mother in every woman to fulfill the purposes of God in the lives of helpless children is my plea to every woman who reads this book. Release the mother in you. When you do, God will release His Grace upon you to accomplish the unimaginable as you invest in a child.

## MOSES, THE DELIVERER

While Moses was in the presence of God on the mountain, he received his commission to return to Egypt. He returned as a man of God with a message for Pharaoh, this time as a deliverer of Israel and not as the son of Pharaoh's daughter. His mission is to deliver God's people from the bondage and slavery of Egypt and set them free from the grips of Pharaoh and his wicked taskmasters. This is what the Lord God instructed Moses to say to Pharaoh:

AND YOU SHALL SAY UNTO PHARAOH, THUS SAITH THE LORD, ISRAEL IS MY SON, EVEN MY FIRSTBORN. AND I SAY UNTO YOU, "LET MY SON GO, THAT HE MAY SERVE ME: AND IF YOU REFUSE TO LET HIM GO, BEHOLD, I WILL KILL YOUR SON, EVEN YOUR FIRSTBORN." EXODUS 4:22-23

The Jews must leave to serve God is the instruction of God to Moses and the command to Pharaoh, "Let my son go." After seeing the demonstration of the power of God, he goes back in the power of God to demonstrate that power through his hands in the presence of the King of Egypt and with a vision to bring Israel, the firstborn out of Egypt. We read in Exodus chapter three the Words of God to Moses. He told him that He had seen the affliction of His people. His decision was to deliver them and bring them out of Egypt and bring them into a large land.

As Moses fulfills his destiny as the deliverer of the Jews, upon his return nothing he does or says would be possible if the women that were divinely placed in his path from birth had not released the mother in them. When a child is nurtured in an environment that allows him or her to line up with the purpose of God, the end result brings glory to God and disgrace and defeat to the kingdom of man and the devil. Thank God that the Pharaoh daughter released the Mother in her to Moses for his destiny.

# CHAPTER 4
# THE CALL TO MOTHERHOOD

As we have examined chapter after chapter, we have learned about all the women who impacted the life of Israel's deliverer, Moses, and their fervency and passion. As a woman you have been called to nurture others, train up your children and positively impact every child God brings your way. The calling of a mother is a lifetime ministry. It is for the rest of your life. Your calling as a mother makes you a beacon of light to the children God has entrusted to you. Visionary mothers such as Jochebed had the foresight to hide her son for three months and relied solely on God for the ability to see clearly into the future. Moses' adopted mother was also wise to hire a nanny to care for her son so he could get the proper care needed as he grows.

Motherhood is about nurturing the next generation of godly parents, pastors, presidents, businessmen, and workers. It is about training our children to have the kind of character that can overcome the many trials that will surely come. Your role as a mother is to lead your children to Christ, to help them learn at His feet and to equip them with the Word of God.

For all the women who read this book, I hope and pray you enjoy your day to day moments with the children in your life, either biological or adopted. Watching my children grow as a father was such an amazing experience, but looking at the face of my wife as she holds and hugs our children is such a beautiful thing. There is nothing as pure as a mother's love for her child. Motherhood is filled with laughter, tears, hugs, tender kisses, correction, discipline, teaching, sleepless nights, hurt, training, fun, messy diaper changing, talking, listening, reading, and so on.

Feelings a father might somehow miss out on because we were not wired that way. Sometimes those moments are ecstatic, like when baby takes his or her first step or first says, "DADA or MAMA," is usually first noticed and most felt by mothers. Sometimes painful moments, like when a child struggles with a particular sin that affects the whole family is also felt most by a mother.

However the moments are filled, they add up to equal a lifetime. It takes God's help to maintain our vision of motherhood. A mother's calling is incomplete without plugging into and connecting with the One who knows all things, Jesus. A mother, as we can see laced throughout the chapters of this book, must have divine wisdom. She must be clothed with humility and patient to raise and nurture her children in the way of the Lord. You have been called to the ministry of motherhood for a divine purpose, it is not by accident, it is by divine appointment. The Lord himself would have made you anything, but he chose to make you a mother, either biologically or through adoption. It is through God's grace you have the ability to conceive, bear, and raise a child.

The essence of motherhood is the appreciation of that role God has designed you for. Throughout the chapters of these books you have seen examples of women who played a role of a mother in the life of Moses, and how that role impacted his destiny. My prayer for all of you is that you become a visionary mother, full of God's wisdom to navigate through the trenches of motherhood, and raise up great men and women in God's kingdom.

A pastor friend of ours got married just before the war in his native land. As a matter of fact, I met him for the first time in the city where we planted our first church, "Unification Town." For some reason, I thought I had seen him before the war. They were displaced, and we took them in for a few weeks. After the dust settled in Kakata, the city where they pastored, we became good friends. Years later, my wife discovered that she and his wife were cousins.

Because of their faithfulness with the Lord's work, they were later transferred to the capital city, Monrovia where they pastored a big church. By this time, they might have been married over six years. As pastors, they also had other people's children living in their home. The pastor's wife, 'mama,' as she was called in their denomination; was and still is a wonderful woman of God who was carrying within her a godly and caring mother with the ability to conceive and bear her own children. She provided for, cared for, and nurtured other children, both physically and spiritually, and as a woman on a mission.

The couple kept praying and believing God for children. We preached at their conventions on countless occasions. We spoke the Word of faith over them on many occasions as the Lord allowed us. We were in agreement with them for many years. One of the church members even gave them his only child, a girl. Though not her own child, yet she mothered her as though she was her biological child.

When the Lord opened the door for the family to relocate to the United States, she brought her as her own child. This is important to note because we know of others that would have returned her to her parents because of the added burden, the distance of moving away from parents or the difficulty in obtaining a visa for a child, which was not theirs biologically. The woman on this mission was not ready to stop at any obstacle but was willing to accomplish her mission, her God-given mission to mother this little girl. Every time we visited their home, we saw a well-mannered child that was cared for and nurtured by a loving mother.

After about ten years of believing and confessing God's Word and mothering other children, God blessed her with two wonderful and smart children, a boy, and a girl. In 2006, while serving as their guest minister at the Christmas Conventions in LA and Arizona, for the first time, I saw the children. I beheld their testimony and the faithfulness of God. I saw the manifestation of the power of God to this couple and to His Word.

Woman, as you read this book, though you do not have your own child, there is a mother in you. You may not feel like it or look like it, but trust God, you are a mother. Look around you and take advantage of opportunities to mother a needy child. Talk to your husband and obtain his approval as the women I mentioned above did. Do it as unto the Lord and to the glory of God. Make it your life's mission, and you will find fulfillment just as God has done for other women who took their mission seriously.

The joy of motherhood is not limited to biological mothers. As a woman who is caring for another's child or children, you are on a mission. The mother in you is best expressed when you begin to care for, nurture, and protect children that you did not give birth to, like Moses' sister, the Egyptian midwives or Pharaoh's daughter, who adopted Moses as her son. Jesus said, if we are able to take of what belongs to another, we will be given our own. We challenge you to allow the mother in you to express herself so that you can experience the joy of motherhood while you mother a child.

## MOTHERHOOD RELEASED

The poem written in the book of Proverbs 31:10-31, has been a great teaching tool to educate women on how to be and what God himself had called them into. You have read what it means to be a mother and the impact you can make in the lives of the children God has blessed you with.

In this chapter, we will learn the specifics from the book of proverbs. From this chapter we can learn specifics on how to utilize some of these lessons to truly walk in your calling as a woman of God and as a mother. Proverbs 31:10-31 reads:

"AN EXCELLENT WIFE, WHO CAN FIND? FOR HER WORTH IS FAR ABOVE JEWELS. THE HEART OF HER HUSBAND TRUSTS IN HER, AND HE WILL HAVE NO LACK OF GAIN. SHE DOES HIM GOOD AND NOT EVIL ALL THE DAYS OF HER LIFE. SHE LOOKS FOR WOOL AND FLAX, AND WORKS WITH HER HANDS

IN DELIGHT. SHE IS LIKE MERCHANT SHIPS; SHE BRINGS HER FOOD FROM AFAR. SHE RISES ALSO WHILE IT IS STILL NIGHT, AND GIVES FOOD TO HER HOUSEHOLD, AND PORTIONS TO HER MAIDENS. SHE CONSIDERS A FIELD AND BUYS IT; FROM HER EARNINGS SHE PLANTS A VINEYARD. SHE GIRDS HERSELF WITH STRENGTH, AND MAKES HER ARMS STRONG. SHE SENSES THAT HER GAIN IS GOOD; HER LAMP DOES NOT GO OUT AT NIGHT. SHE STRETCHES OUT HER HANDS TO THE DISTAFF, AND HER HANDS GRASP THE SPINDLE. SHE EXTENDS HER HAND TO THE POOR; AND SHE STRETCHES OUT HER HANDS TO THE NEEDY. SHE IS NOT AFRAID OF THE SNOW FOR HER HOUSEHOLD, FOR ALL HER HOUSEHOLD ARE CLOTHED WITH SCARLET. SHE MAKES COVERINGS FOR HERSELF; HER CLOTHING IS FINE LINEN AND PURPLE. 23 HER HUSBAND IS KNOWN IN THE GATES, WHEN HE SITS AMONG THE ELDERS OF THE LAND. SHE MAKES LINEN GARMENTS AND SELLS [THEM,] AND SUPPLIES BELTS TO THE TRADESMEN. STRENGTH AND DIGNITY ARE HER CLOTHING, AND SHE SMILES AT THE FUTURE. SHE OPENS HER MOUTH IN WISDOM, AND THE TEACHING OF KINDNESS IS ON HER TONGUE. SHE LOOKS WELL TO THE WAYS OF HER HOUSEHOLD, AND DOES NOT EAT THE BREAD OF IDLENESS. HER CHILDREN RISE UP AND BLESS HER; HER HUSBAND [ALSO,] AND HE PRAISES HER, [SAYING:] 'MANY DAUGHTERS HAVE DONE NOBLY, BUT YOU EXCEL THEM ALL.' CHARM

IS DECEITFUL AND BEAUTY IS VAIN, [BUT] A WOMAN WHO FEARS THE LORD, SHE SHALL BE PRAISED. 31 GIVE HER THE PRODUCT OF HER HANDS, AND LET HER WORKS PRAISE HER IN THE GATES."

The verses express the desire of every man to find an excellent woman, a virtuous woman; woman of moral goodness and propriety combined with the idea of fine manners and culture. According to the poet, this woman is hard to find, and only a few women can achieve the high qualifications needed to be considered virtuous or excellent. She is valuable. A woman of high standards, of high quality; she is rare and precious, she is far above jewels or rubies.

A ruby is a pink to blood-red colored gemstone; the ruby is considered one of the four precious stones, together with the sapphire, the emerald, and the diamond. All natural rubies have imperfections in them, but they are treated with heat in about 3300 F oven. This process cleanses precious rubies from all form of impurities; this is one reason why this woman is so valuable. She is of high quality. Rubies are not valuable just because of their beauty, but because of their rarity. Marble is very pretty, but because it is common it is not considered valuable. The reference to her worth being more than "rubies" explains the heart of God for a woman that is selected and divinely called.

## HONORED (VS 28)

The result of all this that *"Her children rise up and bless her . . . ;"* These children are not forced into this. It is the natural reaction of children who are well reared. They have been taught well so they know how to think wisely and properly. They realize how good of a mother they have and so they bless her. The virtuous woman receives the blessing of her children's praise.

## RESPECTED (VS 29)

She also receives her husband's respect. *Her husband also, and he praises her, saying... "Many daughters have done nobly, But you excel them all."* What wonderful praise for a wife to receive from her husband. He recognizes and tells her that she is a cut above, more than just noble, but excellent, virtuous. Men, do not make the mistake of taking your wife for granted. Encourage her by letting her know how God is using her to bless your life and the good qualities you see in her.

## ACCLAIMED (VS 31)

Finally we find that she is acclaimed by the rest of society as well because of what she produces. *"Give her the product of her hands, and let her works praise her in the gates."* She has brought much blessing to others by what she has done for them. They in turn give praise for it. Her godly character shines in all that she does including the products of her hands. Thus, she is acclaimed.

## MOTHERHOOD IS NOT A HOBBY, IT IS YOUR CALLING.

As a woman you have not been called to collect children as a hobby, but it is what God Himself has called you to be, and has given you the strength and the time for. So many women in our culture today are too selfish to get married or even bear children. You cannot answer the call to motherhood and be selfish, you have to let go of all of your could have's and would have's and lay your life down for God to use. If you are having problems about resting in your call as a mother, then take it to the cross before God. Be ready to sacrifice for your children, put their needs and values ahead of yours; live the gospel as much as you tell them. It is what they see, that they believe.

It is very easy to get discouraged believing no one sees your sacrifice of love. You may get fussy because you seem to be doing everything and no one appreciates it. But you have been called by God to take care of your home, and you will eventually reap what you have sown. Recognize your role in the kingdom; quit trying to be someone God as not called you to be. Focus on seeing your children grow in the admonition of the Lord.

At the heart of every story in the Bible is the love story

of sacrifice that is why I believe that motherhood is the most important occupation in the world, it is filled with sacrificial moments and yet extremely rewarding.

To sum it all up, the calling of a mother was beautifully expressed by a mother, Rachel Jankovic, the author of *Loving the Little Years*;

*"It is about giving up yourself. Lay yourself down. Sacrifice yourself here, now. Cheerfully wipe the nose for the fiftieth time today. Make dinner again for the people who don't like the green beans. Laugh when your plans are thwarted by a vomiting child. Lay yourself down for the people here with you, the people who annoy you, the people who get in your way, the people who take up so much of your time that you can't read anymore. Rejoice in them. Sacrifice for them. Gain that which you cannot lose in them.*

*"It is easy to think you have a heart for orphans on the other side of the world, but if you spend your time at home resenting the imposition your children are on you, you do not. You cannot have a heart for the gospel and fussiness about your life at the same time. You will never make any difference there if you cannot be at peace here. You cannot have a heart for missions but not for the people around you. A true love of the gospel overflows and overpowers. It will be in everything you do, however drab, however simple, however repetitive."*

# ABOUT THE AUTHOR

Rev. S. Musa Korfeh was born on November 14, 1962 unto the union of Mr. and Mrs. Tamba Musa Korfeh, in Firestone, Liberia. He graduated from the Harbel Junior High school in Harbel, Firestone in 1982. In 1983, he moved to Monrovia and enrolled at the St. Patrick's High School and graduated in 1985.

Rev. S. Musa Korfeh earned his Bachelors of Science degree in Theology from the Liberia Assembly of God Bible College in Monrovia, Liberia in 1989. He is a candidate for a master's degree in Theology at the Trinity Bible College and Seminary.

He planted and pastored his first church in Unification Town, Liberia from 1990 to 1992. In late 1992, the Lord called Pastor Korfeh and his family to Freetown, Sierra Leone, where they planted and pastored the Bethel World Outreach Ministries International. By the end of three years, they planted five churches and trained six pastors, all of whom are pastoring today and making significant impact in that nation.

In 1995, Rev. Korfeh was appointed as the first General

Secretary and Missions Director of Bethel World Outreach Ministries International.

Rev. Korfeh, his wife and the children returned to Liberia in 1995 from Sierra Leone. In 1996, he founded and served as the first President of the West Africa School of Missions and Theology and co-pastored Bethel Cathedral of Hope, the ministry's largest and first church in Monrovia, Liberia.

Under his leadership, the West Africa School of Missions and Theology grew and was established in the Republic of Liberia with the purpose of training "Able Ministers" of the New Testament." In April 2000, WASMAT held its first graduation ceremony and awarded Associate Degrees in Theology and Missions. The college is currently training able ministers in Liberia.

Rev. Korfeh is a dynamic and balanced teacher of the Word of God, a missionary at heart with an Apostolic Anointing for the nations. He has ministered in many countries around the world, including Liberia, the Republic of Sierra Leone, Guinea, the Ivory Coast, Kenya, Tanzania, South Africa, Mali, Cameroon, Canada, Angola, and the USA. He is the founder and senior pastor of Bethel World Outreach Church: The City of Power, a growing ministry in Houston, Texas. He recently planted two other churches in Vancouver, B.C., Canada, and Arizona.

Rev. Korfeh is the founder of Power Ministries International, a missions' ministry for the body of Christ to reach the nations of Africa and third world countries with the Gospel in the demonstration of the Holy Ghost and Power. He ministers and operates in the gifts of the Holy Spirit as the Spirit leads him. He is an experienced deliverance minister and has brought deliverance and healing to many around the world, including the USA. Power Ministries International was launched on April 12, 2008 in Houston, Texas.

He currently serves as the First Assistant Presiding Prelate (Assistant Bishop) to the Presiding Prelate of Bethel World Outreach Ministries International, Inc., Bishop Darlingston G. Johnson.

Rev. S. Musa Korfeh is married to Rev. Farmah Jeraldine Korfeh. They are blessed with six lovely children, Patience, Martina, Pearl-muscynette, Musa, Darlingston, and Farmah, Jr.

# NOTES